PRESENTED TO

_____

FROM

_____

He is not here.

He has risen from the dead

as he said he would.

MATTHEW 28:6

PUBLISHER'S ACKNOWLEDGMENT
The publisher wishes to acknowledge that the text for *Resurrection Morning* appeared originally in *Tell Me the Story*, written by Max Lucado and illustrated by Ron DiCianni. Special thanks to Ron DiCianni for the idea and vision behind the creation of the "Tell Me" series. Look for more stories in the series—*Tell Me the Secrets, Tell Me the Truth, Tell Me the Promises,* and *Tell Me Why,* all published by Crossway Books—at your local bookstore.

Cover and interior art adapted from the film *Resurrection*,
produced by Tom Newman, Impact Productions
Design: Kirk DouPonce, UDG│DesignWorks, www.udgdesignworks.com
First printing 1992, new edition 2004
Printed in Italy

LIBRARY OF CONGRESS CATALOGING-IN-PUBLICATION DATA.
Lucado, Max.
Resurrection morning/Max Lucado.
p. cm.
ISBN 1-58134-547-X (HC : alk. paper)
1. Jesus Christ—Resurrection—Fiction. 2. Centurion at the Crucifixion (Biblical figure)—Fiction. 3. Bible. N.T. —History of Biblical events—Fiction. I. Title.
PS3562.U225R47 2004
813'.54—dc22   2003017432

PBI   14   13   12   11   10   09   08   07   06   05   04
15   14   13   12   11   10   9   8   7   6   5   4   3   2   1

For

Marie Shipp

and

Maria Dutton

May the promise of
resurrection morning
gild your days.

MAX LUCADO

RESURRECTION MORNING

CROSSWAY BOOKS · WHEATON, ILLINOIS

A DIVISION OF GOOD NEWS PUBLISHERS

Tell it again, you say? Tell it again? I've told you all I know. I've even told what I don't know."

"But some are just arriving. They haven't heard what you saw. Tell us again."

The heavy door opened and shut quickly as two more men entered the small room. Claudius supposed this was a storage room, but he wasn't sure. It was too dark. The only light was a slit of afternoon sunshine creeping through an opening in the wooden shutters and streaking across the faces of the listeners.

The group numbered fifteen, maybe twenty—
about as many men as women. A few men were
shaven, most bearded. A few asked questions. A
few shook their heads. All sat with eyes fixed
on the young soldier whose story they longed
to hear but didn't know whether to believe.

Claudius took a breath and began his story
again. "I wasn't supposed to work that night.
I'd worked over the Sabbath and was tired. In fact,
I had been on duty since Friday morning."

"I remember your face." The voice belonged to a woman sitting on the floor. "You were on the hill."

"I was assigned the Golgotha detail a month ago." A grumble went up from the group. Claudius defended himself. "I didn't ask for it. I was given it."

Emotion was thick in the room, but then someone was urging, "Go on, finish the story!"

Claudius again shifted his weight. He would never have imagined himself in a room full of Jews.

The contrast between his trimmed hair and short uniform and their beards and robes only added to his discomfort. He eyed his spear on the floor at his feet. His Roman shield leaned against the adobe wall. Coming here was a dangerous move.

He had been uneasy ever since he had arrived in Jerusalem a few months back. Certainly wasn't his choice of a place to serve, but when Rome sends, a soldier obeys. Besides, he told himself, a year in a peaceful outpost couldn't be too bad.

Wrong, Jerusalem was far from peaceful.

The Jews hated the soldiers. The soldiers distrusted the Jews. If it wasn't the priests' complaints, it was the zealots' riots. Forget casual strolls down the street keeping peace. Jerusalem was a hotbed of anger. Anger at Rome. Anger at the world.

They called themselves the people of God. Some nation of God! No navy. Puny army. No emperor. Just a temple, a Torah, and some strange rules about the Sabbath. Claudius had been trained to respect strength and size—neither of which he found here.

Until last night. What he saw last night he'd never seen in Rome or anywhere else. When he told his officers about it, they told him to keep quiet. He couldn't. He had to have some answers. So he came here. These people wanted answers, too. So they let him in.

They were easy to find. Every soldier in the city knew where they were hiding—the upper room of the large white corner house. It was the same place they had met last week when He was still here.

One by one they had drifted back to the room—each entering with a knock on the door and a shameful nod. When Claudius learned how they had run away and left Him alone, he was amazed that they had returned. "Why are you still here then?" he had asked. "Why don't you go home?"

"If you'd seen Him do what we've seen Him do, you would stay, too," a disciple explained.

"Sounds like he has," added another.

For by now they all knew what had happened at the tomb. Or better, they knew something had happened at the tomb. No one quite knew how to explain it. Claudius picked up his story where he'd left off.

"When I first saw Him being led up the hill, I noticed He was different. He didn't demand we let Him go. He didn't shout or resist. And when we hammered the spike into His hand—" Claudius paused, wondering if he should have mentioned this. An encouraging nod from one of the women told him to continue. "When we placed the spike in His hand, He held His hand still. He didn't fight."

"When we placed

the spike in His hand,

He held His hand still.

He didn't fight."

"Sounds like something He would do," a man in the back stated. Several nodded in agreement.

"He never seemed angry." Claudius's voice grew softer as he continued. "He never blamed anyone. People were cursing and laughing at Him, but not once did I see His eyes lose their calm."

No one moved as Claudius spoke. When he had shared these events with his superiors earlier in the day, they had scoffed. It didn't matter to the Romans how Jesus had acted. But it mattered to these people. They wanted to know every detail. For the first time Claudius felt a camaraderie with his listeners—a camaraderie based on a fascination with one Man.

He continued, "'Forgive them,' I heard him say. And when He spoke, I looked up. He was looking at me. His face was a mask of blood and spit. But He was praying for me."

"'Forgive them,'

I heard him say.

And when He spoke,

I looked up.

He was looking at me."

The only movement in the room was the nodding of heads.

"After the crucifixion I helped lower the body and lay it on the ground. I waited as these women—" He motioned to several near the front. "I waited as they prepared the body, and then I saw that it was placed in the tomb."

"I thought my day was over. I took four men to close the grave's opening with a huge stone. When we turned to leave, word came that Pilate and the temple leaders were nervous that someone would steal the body. We were told to seal the tomb and stand guard all night."

"There were several of us; so we built a fire and took turns. I was the first to sleep. When they woke me for my turn, it was an hour before dawn. The night was black—as black as any night I can remember. The moon was small, and the stars were hidden by the clouds.

"I stood on one side. Another soldier stood on the other. He laughed about how easy it was to guard a tomb. Not often does a soldier get guard duty in a cemetery. Maybe we dozed off, but at first I thought I was dreaming. The ground began to shake—violently. It shook so hard I fell to the ground. Rocks fell from the walls behind us. Sparks flew from the fire. The soldiers asleep on the ground jumped up. I know they were standing because when the light hit them, I could see their faces like it was broad daylight."

The rock rolled back,

and the light roared out.

A burst of fire

with no heat.

"What light?" someone asked.

"You tell me!" Claudius demanded. "Where did that light come from? The rock rolled back, and the light roared out. A burst of fire with no heat. A gust of wind blew from the tomb, put out the fire, knocked us back, and the next thing I knew, the tomb was empty. I looked at the soldiers. They were stunned. About that time these two women appeared."

"That's when we saw the angel!" Mary blurted. "He was sitting on the rock! He told us that Jesus was not there. He told us that..."

She hesitated, knowing her words would be hard to believe. "He told us that Jesus is no longer dead!"

Her words rang in the room like a peal of a bell. No one dared to speak. Finally one did. A clean-shaven younger man said softly, but firmly, "Just like He said he would."

"You mean, He said He would do this?" Claudius asked.

"More than once. But we didn't understand. We didn't believe. Until today."

"John," one of the women asked the man speaking, "you were there. You went to the tomb. Is that what you saw?"

"Peter and I saw the tomb. We saw it open and empty. But we didn't see Jesus."

Once again the room was quiet. Then Claudius broke the silence. "I have a question.

I've told you what you wanted to know. Now you tell me what I want to know. This has been on my mind all weekend. It's been on my heart ever since I struck the nail into Jesus' hand. Who is this man? Who is this Jesus?"

If any head had hung before, it lifted at this moment. If any thoughts had wandered, they wandered no more.

"Is there any doubt?" Mary said. Her eyes were bright. She jumped to her feet as she spoke.

"I saw Him! I saw Him risen from the dead. He is who He said He is. He is the Son of God!"

With the statement the room broke into chaos.

"Impossible!"

"No, she's right. Let her speak!"

"Why did He let them kill Him if He is the Son of God?"

"It doesn't make sense."

"What doesn't make sense is why you can't believe!"

Claudius was silent. What he was hearing, he could not handle. But what he had seen at the grave, he could not deny. He leaned over and put his elbows on his knees and buried his face in his hands. Thoughts rumbled in his head. He was so intent that he didn't notice the sudden silence. Stillness reigned for several seconds before he raised his head. A light filled the room. He looked at the door and the window; they were still closed.

Faces that had been cast in shadows now beamed. All eyes stared in his direction—not at him but behind him. But before he could turn to see what they were seeing, a hand was on his shoulder. When Claudius turned to look at the hand, he found the answer for his heart.

The hand was pierced.

When Claudius turned

to look at the hand,

he found the answer

for his heart.

The hand was pierced.

"I am the resurrection and the life.
Whoever believes in me, though he die,
yet shall he live....

JOHN 11:25-26, ESV